Are You Ready for Heaven?

The Best Is Yet to Come!

T.E. Bird

Titles may be purchased in bulk for educational, business, fundraising or sales promotional use. For information, please email TEBirdBooks@gmail.com.

Table of Contents

Dedication

To My Family

I love you and always will.

You are my "CONNECT4".

Wife + (Mother x 2) = Abundant Blessings!

Thank you for the joy that you bring to my life and for making this possible.

Acknowledgements

To the Early Birds

I love your hearts for God.

You are powerful prayer warriors!

5 Birds @ 6am = Ladies Bible Study for 20+ years.

About the Author

T.E. Bird lives in England and attends the International Community Church (ICC) in Surrey (http://www.icc-uk.org). She moved to England with her husband, Kevin, from Houston, Texas, in 2004, along with their two children, Brian and Katherine. They are dual citizens – British and American. Having made the decision to follow Christ at 9 years of age, T.E. has been a lifelong Christian. This book was written after discussions with a nice young man called James, who was apathetic to Christianity. For all who are uncertain about your eternal destination, I pray you are blessed by turning each page, as you come to know Jesus Christ. To God be the Glory!

Introduction

"Now to him who is able to do immeasurably more than all we ask or imagine, according to his power that is at work within us. Amen."

- **Ephesians 3:20**

This book is meant to introduce you to a true companion, lover and friend, who promises to be with you through all of life's ups and downs. It will challenge your perspective on why time is of the essence for you to make a decision, which will change the rest of your life. This is where our journey begins for today and forevermore because the best is yet to come by knowing Jesus Christ!

Chapter 1: Are You Ready for Departure?

In March 1981, Carl McCunn paid a pilot to take him to a remote lake 225 miles northeast of Fairbanks, Alaska. He had meticulously planned every detail of what was going to be an eight-month adventure of camping and capturing wildlife on film. The 35-year-old carefully packed 500 rolls of film, 1400 pounds of provisions, two rifles and a shotgun. McCunn had sent three maps with his campsite marked to some friends and his father, but he was not clear about his exact itinerary or when he would return.

McCunn had told his father not to be concerned if he did not return at the end of the summer because he might stay later in the season. Although McCunn thought he had arranged for the pilot to return for him in August, he had apparently never confirmed this departure. In January 1982, when he did not return, McCunn's friends and family became concerned enough to ask the authorities to begin a search for him. On February 2, 1982, State Troopers landed at the lake to find McCunn's campsite. They found his body next to a 100-page diary detailing his hope someone would arrive in time.

None of us gets to choose whether we slip away peacefully in the night, ravaged by a disease that we neither wanted nor deserved or taken by an accident we never saw coming. We must be ready for the eventuality of death. Given that we will never know the time of our death or the circumstances, we need to be confident we will go to heaven when we die. If not, then time is of the essence to make this decision because life can be unpredictable. Let's look at someone who, unfortunately, waited too late.

In the Bible, there is a parable in Luke 16:19-31, about a rich man and a beggar named Lazarus, who waited outside of the rich man's gate for any scraps of food. This is the only parable where our Lord gives us a contrast between this world and the next. It is also unusual since this is the only parable to use a name for the character, Lazarus, but all references related to the rich man are generic descriptions of someone being self-indulgent. This is likely presented this way because Jesus knew many others in this world would be self-absorbed by wealth and material possessions.

When they both died, the rich man went to hell, but the poor beggar, Lazarus, went to heaven. The rich man asked Abraham, an early patriarch in the Bible, if he would send Lazarus to go warn his family about the torment of hell. Abraham replied they had Moses and all the rest of the prophets to warn them. If they would not listen to Moses and the prophets, they would not be persuaded if someone rose from the dead and told them. Therefore, the request for Lazarus to go back was denied.

What do we learn from this passage? Unless you make the decision to follow Jesus Christ, you are at risk of having the same fate as the rich man, which was to spend eternity in hell in a constant state of torment. Secondly, the choice to follow Jesus must be made on this side of heaven. Otherwise, like the rich man, you will not be given an opportunity to go back to warn others or to reverse your own eternal destination. It also clearly teaches us that the dead cannot communicate with the living or be allowed to change their minds. And finally, it teaches that we must prioritise helping the poor and love our neighbours.

With this parable in mind, have you considered your own departure, i.e. death? What do you believe will happen after you die? Unfortunately, Carl McCunn never returned from the Alaskan wilderness. Tragically, he had done everything else except plan his departure. When his food provisions ran out during the winter, he left an entry in his diary that said, "I think I should have used more foresight about arranging my departure." [1] [2]

You see, death does not discriminate based upon whether we are young, old, rich or poor. It can be fast and immediate or a slow decline over months or years. Before you experience physical death, I pray you encounter Jesus in a way you are convinced of who He is and what He has done. Then, you can have a vibrant, flourishing relationship with Jesus, who will give you purpose, meaning and a new identity. More than anything, I desire for you to know the Jesus I know because then, you will live a life filled with

---

[1] Thompson, E. (2018). Death in the Wild – Carl McCunn. An article by Emily Thompson. Morbidology. Retrieved from: https://morbidology.com/death-in-the-wild-carl-mccunn/

[2] The New York Times. (2021). *Left In Wilds, Man Penned Dying Record.* Retrieved from: https://www.nytimes.com/1982/12/19/us/left-in-wilds-man-penned-dying-record.html

promise and eternal hope. Let's explore how we can be ready for our departure!

Chapter 2: What Is Required for Eternal Life?

Sixteen years ago, we moved to England, and at that time, the International Community Church had an evening service in a little village called Thorpe, at a beautiful, 12th-century church. A friend of ours was visiting from the States and joined us for the evening service. Usually, the sermons were on a topic or involved studying a book of the Bible, but that evening, the pastor dedicated the entire service to the foundational tenets of being a Christian and our need to believe in Jesus Christ to inherit everlasting life. We arrived home and were cleaning up from dinner when our friend turned to us and said, "Surely, you don't believe what the Pastor said tonight about Jesus." We replied that we did and asked her if she thought that she was going to heaven. Our friend went on to explain, "Yes, because I am a good person and try to do what's right." Unfortunately, there was a flaw in our friend's logic because to be declared "good", there must be a standard to be measured against.

God's standard is holy and perfect, and absolutely none of us measure up to that standard based upon our thoughts or actions. Like my friend, it is easy to deceive myself into believing that I have been "good enough" when compared to someone who might have committed really hideous, torturous crimes. However, would I be "good enough" to get into heaven if I was being compared to someone who had devoted their whole life to serving God? All of a sudden, I don't look so "good" if I am compared to Mother Teresa's devotion to helping the marginalised poor, sick and destitute in Calcutta, India. Would I be "good" if I am compared to Billy Graham, the prominent televangelist who held crusades all over the world, with 3.2 million people responding to his invitation to follow Christ over his decades of ministry? [3]

---

[3] Shellnutt, K. (2021). Billy Graham's Death Leads 10,000 to Pray for Salvation. Retrieved 2 April 2021, from: https://www.christianitytoday.com/news/2018/march/billy-graham-death-10000-pray-for-salvation-bgea-memorial.html

The Bible says none of us could ever be good enough to earn our salvation, so thankfully, as Christians, we do not need to perform certain rituals or keep certain laws to earn our way into heaven. Works and efforts will not assure any of us of everlasting life because our eternal life is not based upon self-reliance.

This flawed logic of being "good enough" is commonly referred to as "works righteousness", which means that each of us must obey a prescribed set of practices to avoid judgement and earn eternal life. Jesus teaches about being considered "good" when he answers a young ruler. In Mark 10:17-18, the Scripture says,

"As Jesus started on His way, a man ran up and knelt before Him. 'Good Teacher', he asked, 'what must I do to inherit eternal life?'

'Why do you call me good?' Jesus replied, 'No one is good except God alone'."

First of all, notice the casual way in which the young man approaches Jesus. The young ruler clearly does not acknowledge Jesus as a deity with the use of 'Good Teacher'. The young man used the word "good," as though Jesus was merely a good teacher, in much the same way that certain Jewish rabbis had distinguished themselves as effective teachers. [4]

It also appears that the young ruler believes that eternal life is a matter of works or deserving, i.e. "works righteousness", rather than having a relationship with Jesus Christ.

Eternal life is not something we earn by using a checklist; our salvation is solely based upon what Jesus Christ has already done for each of us. The bottom line is no one will enter heaven unless they believe in Jesus Christ. It says in Acts 4:12, "There is salvation in no one else, for there is no other name under heaven given among men by which we must be saved." All people "have sinned and fallen short of the glory of God" (Rom 3:23), and the penalty for our sin is death (Romans 6:23). We all are sinners because we are incapable of living up to God's holy and perfect standard by relying on our own merits or efforts. However, Jesus Christ loved us enough to die on the cross in our place to pay the

---

[4] The New York Times. (2021). *Left In Wilds, Man Penned Dying Record.* Retrieved from: https://www.nytimes.com/1982/12/19/us/left-in-wilds-man-penned-dying-record.html

penalty for our sins (Rom 5:8). It is only through our belief in Jesus Christ that we can receive forgiveness of our sins and eternal life with God, our Heavenly Father.

You might be wondering what we have to do to accept this free gift of eternal life. Well, you must believe in Jesus Christ. As it says in John 3:16, "For God loved each of us so much that he gave His one and only Son, that whoever believes in him shall not perish but have eternal life." To have eternal life, we have to admit that we are sinners and accept what Christ did through dying on the cross. Christ has paid the price for all our sins – past, present and future. Yes, did you catch that? Even our future sins that we have not committed yet are covered because Christ's death paid the price for our sins, once and for all.

Saving faith is unmerited and undeserved by us but freely given by God's grace so that we might have eternal life. We do not provide ourselves with faith, for it is a gift of God, which is referenced in Ephesians 2:8-9, "For it is by grace you have been saved, through faith – and this not from yourselves, it is the gift of God – not by works, so that no one can boast." It's more than just believing that Jesus exists. It means being willing to rely on Christ, based upon his claims, his words and his actions. We all have sinned and deserve the wrath of God. The penalty of sin is not only physical death but eternal separation from God. More than anything, we need to be declared righteous before God instead of guilty. The whole reason that Jesus came was to stand in place of sinners so that we could be declared righteous before a Holy God through our faith in Him.

You see, salvation is not merely trying to be "good". Saving faith means that we believe who Jesus says He was, that is, the Son of God. It means we believe that he really can do what he says he can do. It also implies that we are willing to put our faith, trust and reliance upon Jesus Christ, who died in our place and for our sins. It means being willing to turn away from our sin and submit to His authority in every aspect of our lives. As Christians, we never earn our way to heaven or ever expect our own good deeds to be enough. Rather, it is only through our faith in Jesus Christ that we are guaranteed everlasting life.

I love how Tim Keller clarifies the difference between works based religions and God's saving grace. Most other religions say, "I obey – therefore I'm accepted." Those types of religions believe that we must be following "works-based" rules to earn our way to eternal life. However, the Gospel says, "I'm accepted – therefore I obey". [5]

Being Christians, our obedience flows out of our love and gratitude for what God has done on our behalf through Jesus Christ. Our good works, here on earth, do not merit or assure us of salvation, but they certainly demonstrate the sincerity of our faith. Friends, we are saved by faith alone, but it should always be accompanied by the good works in our church, community and families.

In the Gospel of Matthew, Jesus was asked for the greatest commandments, and His reply reflects what our priorities in life should be. In Matthew 22:37-39, Jesus replied: "Love the Lord your God with all your heart and with all your soul and with all your mind." This is the first and greatest commandment. And the second is: "Love your neighbour as yourself." As devoted Christians, we love God and want to serve Him; therefore, His love should flow through us to love our neighbours.

---

[5] Kellier, T. (2021). Retrieved 2 April 2021, from: https://www.reddit.com/r/Christianity/comments/zsgfb/religion_operates_on_the_principle_of_i/

We are the hands and feet of God in this world so that we can show Christ's love to our neighbours. We aren't serving our neighbours to earn special privileges with God or earn our way to heaven. God loves us unconditionally and created us in His image. He is eager and waiting to have an intimate, personal relationship with each of us. We love because He first loved us. Out of this love and devotion to Him comes our desire to serve. Friends, that's exactly how His love flows through us to love our neighbours!

Many of us may volunteer for all kinds of organisations or clubs, but this is not necessarily a service. Serving is much more than merely volunteering our time. For example, we may volunteer our time for an organisation that has a mission that we want to support or help. However, when we serve, our primary motive is to be able to demonstrate the love of Christ in our communities, churches and families. Serving is "an attitude of noticing, caring about and helping others. It is an inward feeling of loving and caring about the welfare of all those around us, caring about their salvation as much as our own." [6]

Jesus came to this world to save, but He also came to serve. From His miracles, we know that Christ noticed, cared and helped many people. Over and over, Jesus had compassion for all kinds of people and in a myriad of situations. He healed the lame. He fed the hungry. He resurrected the dead. He spent time with the outcasts. Ultimately, He died for the forgiveness of our sins so that we might be declared righteous before God in heaven.

You may be wondering where this eternal home called heaven is where Christians go after they die (Philippians 1:21-33)? The Bible tells us that our heavenly home is a city built by God (Hebrews 11:10) and more glorious than we could ever imagine, with no pain, suffering or tears. It is God's dwelling place (Psalms 33:13) and where Christ is today (Acts 1:11). "Most of us have heard that heaven is a place where the streets are paved with gold, the gates are made of pearl, and the walls made of precious jewels. Those

---

[6] The Two Greatest Commandments. (2021). Retrieved 2 April 2021, from: http://www.spokanecares.org/two-greatest-commandments.php

images come from Revelation 21, which offers us the most extended picture of heaven in the entire Bible." [7] God has chosen to reveal some descriptions about heaven in the Bible, but much remains unknown until we arrive at our glorious eternal home.

I love how Max Lucado, a Christian evangelist and prolific author, says, "your final hour will be your finest hour" because there's no doubt that heaven will be more amazing than we have ever imagined. What is required for eternal life? Belief in Jesus Christ will open the door to heaven and friends; it will be our finest hour!

---

[7] Neely, D. (2021). You Brought Pavement to Heaven? - Encouragement Café - June 23 - Encouragement Café. Retrieved 2 April 2021, from: https://www.oneplace.com/devotionals/encouragement-cafe/you-brought-pavement-to-heaven-encouragement-cafe-june-23-11828587.html

Chapter 3: Blessed Assurance, Jesus Is Mine!

Three of our family were seated on a small EMB-145 plane, taking us from Chicago, Illinois and onto Syracuse, New York. We were heading to Syracuse because our daughter was graduating from university the next day. The Captain came on the public address system and asked for volunteers to give up their seats because the flight was oversold. Nada! No one got out of their seats because most of the customers were headed to the graduation in Syracuse. The Captain asked a second time, increasing the cash incentive being offered, warning us that if needed, they would have to remove someone from the flight to make room for another pilot who had to be taken to Syracuse. Again, no one jumped at the chance. In a few minutes, the ground gate crew entered the plane, walked past me and my husband and stopped at our son's row. They escorted our 27-year-old son off the plane, only briefly reassuring us that he would be re-routed through Philadelphia, Pennsylvania and onto Syracuse later that evening.

My husband and I flew onto Syracuse while our son was delayed further in Chicago. By the time our son's flight was due to arrive in Philadelphia, he was going to miss his connection, with no more flights going to Syracuse that evening. Therefore, as an alternative plan, the airline booked our son from Chicago on the last flight leaving to Rochester, New York, which was the closest that they could get him to Syracuse. By that time, my husband and I had checked into a Syracuse hotel with a booking for two rooms expecting our son to arrive. In the middle of the night, my husband made a 170-mile round car journey to pick up our son and returned to Syracuse at 4 am, in time for the graduation ceremony to be held at 9 am. As you can imagine, it was not a restful night before a long day of graduation festivities. Apparently, what led the airline to select our son to send him on the connecting flight, was that he was flying on "freebie" air miles instead of purchasing a full-price ticket.

Our son did not have the full price privileges, so he was diverted to an entirely different route and end destination. However, the passengers with a full-price ticket were allowed to continue on the direct flight. Similarly, we will need full price privileges to enter the gates of heaven someday, and that can only be secured through believing in Jesus Christ and what He has done on our behalf.

Whether planned or accidental, there is no reversing death, and life as we know it will come to an end. Modern-day medicine and exercise may prolong the eventuality of each of us physically dying, but ultimately death will come, unless, of course, Jesus Christ returns for the second coming, as the Bible teaches us.

Before death occurs, we need to be confident about our eternal destination. The Bible characterises the human race as being "saved" or "lost", based upon whether you believe in the saving grace of Jesus Christ. Upon death, there will be two different destinations, depending on whether you have surrendered your life to follow Jesus. One destination will be with Jesus Christ in paradise or the other in perpetual torment in a place called hell. As Romans 6:23 says, "For the wages of sin is death, but the free gift of God is eternal life in Christ Jesus our Lord." Not much in this world is offered for free. However, eternal life is a free gift through God's amazing grace, but only if we believe in Jesus Christ.

I was 9 years old at the time, waiting in the foyer of the Park Plaza Nursing Home in Whitney, Texas, for my mother to get off from work. My mother was an administrator who did accounting and payroll work. There was a visiting pastor who normally came once a week in the afternoons to conduct a church service for the patients. A lot of people had gathered to attend the service, including some ambulatory patients, along with a few others in wheelchairs and, of course, me.

Although I don't remember his name, the pastor's chosen words had a profound, lasting impact on my life. In a very loving manner, the pastor gave his message, and at the end, he said, "if you do not know the day or the season when you made a decision to ask Jesus to be your Lord and Saviour, then you need to evaluate whether you have". He grabbed my attention by that closing statement and by inviting each of us to reflect on our own faith.

I thought to myself, do I know the day when I became a Christian? Unfortunately, no! Since I couldn't remember an exact day, I tried to think of a season in life where I asked Jesus to become my Lord and Saviour? Again, sadly, I had to answer "no"! My parents had always taken me to church; therefore, I was familiar with the stories of Jesus. My grandfather was a Methodist Minister, so I grew up in a Christian home. I had spent my early summers going to

Vacation Bible Schools at the local Methodist and Baptist Churches. However, I knew in my heart that I had never made a personal decision for Jesus Christ to be my Saviour.

I said nothing at the end of the service, but all the way home, I pondered over the pastor's words. I desperately wanted the assurance that came with salvation. That night, on Friday, December 22nd, 1972, right before Christmas, I dedicated my life to follow Jesus Christ. That was my moment of believing in and accepting Jesus as my Lord and Saviour.

Ever since that point, it has been an incredible journey with Jesus. Over many decades, I have seen Jesus at work in my life and in the lives of others. Who is Jesus to me? Jesus is a healer when all odds and prognosis seem impossible. He is a restorer so that my past sins no longer define my future. He is a comforter when death gives way to the promise of eternal life. He is a companion when loneliness is replaced by a meaningful relationship with Him. He is a protector when fear and danger are present. He is a provider when financial uncertainty becomes new opportunities at just the right time and place. Most of all, He is my Lord and Saviour, and I pray that He is yours too.

Frances Jane "Fanny" Crosby could have been bitter about her fate, but she became one of the most prolific hymnists of all time, with more than 8000 hymns and gospel songs under her belt. She had tragically lost her sight as a baby after a mistreated eye infection. Later, her mother was widowed at the age of 21 when her father died. While her mother worked to make a living, Fanny's grandmother was very instrumental in raising her, making sure she was grounded in faith with a strong knowledge of the Bible. The lyrics of Mrs Crosby's 1873 hymn called *Blessed Assurance* reflect the confidence that she had in her salvation and serve as a beautiful illustration of the tenets of the Christian faith.

Blessed assurance, Jesus is mine!
Oh, what a foretaste of glory divine!
Heir of salvation, purchase of God,
Born of His Spirit, washed in His blood

Chorus:

This is my story, this is my song,
Praising my Saviour all the day long;
This is my story, this is my song,
Praising my Saviour all the day long [8]

The lyrics remind us that this world is only the foretaste of the glory that will come when we get to heaven. By saying "Yes" to follow Christ, we become a child of God and joint-heir with Jesus. We do not have to work to earn our eternal salvation because by virtue of having faith in Christ, we are considered joint-heirs with Him.

---

[8] Fanny Crosby: America's Hymn Queen. (2021). Retrieved 3 April 2021, from: https://www.christianity.com/church/church-history/timeline/1801-1900/fanny-crosby-americas-hymn-queen-11630385.html

All that is rightfully granted to Jesus is ours through His sacrifice. Two thousand years ago, we were purchased by His blood on the cross and became rightful heirs to the kingdom of heaven through our faith in Jesus Christ. [9]

When believers someday stand before God in heaven, our sins will be covered by the purity of the sinless, blameless blood of Jesus Christ. This is God's grace at work, in that we deserved death for our sins. When God forgives our sins, He completely forgets them. That means He will no longer hold our sins against us per Hebrew 8:12. Our sins were nailed to the cross when Christ died for us, but what does it mean to be "in Christ"?

According to 2 Corinthians 5:17b, "If anyone is in Christ, he is a new creation; the old has gone, the new has come!" Only God can bring about a new creation by changing us spiritually, which is what Fanny Crosby meant by being "born of the spirit". This means completely changing our allegiance and intentions to become more like

---

[9] Kenneth Copeland Ministries. 2020. Kenneth Copeland Ministries - 3 Reasons Why You Are An Heir Of God. [online] Available at: https://www.kcm.org/real-help/faith/learn/3-reasons-why-you-are-heir-god [Accessed 23 June 2020]

Christ instead of being self-absorbed. As God changes us, Galatians 5:22-23 says that our lives will begin to reflect and value the fruits of the spirit, such as love, joy, peace, patience, kindness, goodness, faithfulness, gentleness, and self-control. As a new creation, we will not be perfect, but we will have a genuine desire to love and honour all that God wants and will be convicted to completely turn away from our sin.

And finally, as Ms Crosby's hymn says, we are "washed in His blood". This means Jesus paid the price for all of humanity's sins by His blood and sacrifice on the cross. If you have asked God to forgive your sins and made the decision to follow Jesus, then you will have eternal life, sometimes referred to as being "in Christ". As such, according to Romans 8:1, "Therefore, there is now no condemnation for those who are in Christ Jesus". This means God's wrath for sin was justified by Christ on our behalf. When God looks at us, who are "in Christ", He only sees the perfection of Jesus and not our own flawed works or efforts, which could never be good enough to earn our way into heaven.

When Christ died on the cross, Matthew 27:51 tells us, “The veil of the temple was torn in two from top to bottom”. This is incredibly significant because, in the Old Testament days, the priests were the only ones allowed to enter the Holy of Holies in the temple. Once per year, the priests would visit the temple on the Day of Atonement to make sacrifices for the Israelites’ sins under the old covenant. The animals used in the sacrifices had to be the best of the herd, unblemished. The sprinkled blood symbolically covered the sins and shielded the sinner from God’s judgment.

However, when Christ died, He ushered in the new covenant, forgiving our sins and giving us free access to God. This means that we no longer have to pray, confess, or try to acquire fellowship through anyone else because each of us now has direct access to God, which was represented by the tearing of the temple veil. Every day we can pray and enjoy a personal relationship with God, who loves and cares for each of us.

You see, our assurance of everlasting life comes from what Jesus did on the cross and not based upon our own righteousness. Jesus gave up His life on the cross for you and me. Hanging on the cross, Jesus said in John 19:30, “It is finished… And bowing His head, He gave up his spirit." Notice that Jesus willingly gave up His life in that world-changing moment to pay the price for our sins. It was not taken from Him by the Roman soldiers, but He willingly, consciously, laid down His life to be the sacrifice for our sins. Jesus was sinless, blameless, and therefore, He was the perfect sacrifice to atone for our sins, once and for all. Just as prophesized, on the 3rd day, Jesus rose from the grave. He overcame death to assure us of everlasting life in heaven, for all who believe in Him.

If we repent of our sins and have faith in the atoning work of Christ, then our physical death will usher us immediately into the glorious presence of God in heaven for all of eternity. In essence, we are given "full price privileges" to enter heaven based upon who Christ is and what He has done. That's the Good News of Jesus Christ – for you and for me!

Chapter 4: Jesus and the Bible – Fact or Fiction?

All of us have perspectives that have been formed by what we have been taught and experienced. I grew up in a small town in Central Texas and lived in the same house until I went to university at 18 years of age. My parents lived through World War II when money was extremely scarce. Growing up, they produced all of our meat and vegetables on a farm. We canned vegetables during the summer, so we could eat them during the winter. Springtime was spent planting the garden, with potatoes always being planted with the "eyes up". We washed bread bags and aluminium foil so that they could be re-used. We never went on extravagant holidays and rarely, ever went out to eat. Both of my parents worked all their life and meticulously saved any extra money they could. My parents were Christians, so we always attended church on Sundays, ensconced on the 2nd row to the back pew. My twin brother and I were regulars at the church youth group. We both played the piano from the Methodist hymnal because we never had any sheet music. All of these experiences helped shape my worldview, including my beliefs and spiritual growth.

With all my heart, I believe that the Bible is God's inspired Holy Word. It is not fabricated stories but a consolidation of 66 books written by dozens of authors that beautifully and convincingly share God's plan for salvation through His Son, Jesus Christ. It is divided into two sections – the Old Testament, which points us to Christ's coming and the New Testament tells us of His arrival and what is to come in the future. From the Bible, we know Jesus performed many miracles, such as healing the sick, turning water into wine, enabling the lame to walk, feeding multitudes, casting out demons and restoring the dead to life. Every one of these miracles was intended to establish His identity and demonstrate His power.

I recognise that many other people have no background in Christianity, so you may not share my belief that the early writings documented the greatest man ever to live, Jesus Christ. I completely accept that if you believe that Jesus is just another ordinary guy, a Jewish carpenter, none of this really makes any difference. However, if Jesus is the Son of God, the Messiah, then your eternal life is at stake. As

Christians, we "believe that Jesus is the Christ, the Son of God, and that by believing you have life in His name." (John 20:31)

When police investigate a crime, they look for evidence that suggests the people, places, and events happened as they were told or recorded by witnesses. They look for people who are, ideally, eyewitnesses because they are more credible in making a case for what happened. The same holds true for discovering the truth about Jesus. The more information that is available from eyewitnesses or available in the same century that Jesus lived, when eyewitnesses could have refuted the facts, the more reliable it is considered to be.

Before you dismiss this as a complete waste of time, I want to share some of the archaeological evidence that confirms that the people, places and events happened in the Bible. The evidence is overwhelmingly detailed and would hardly qualify as easy bedtime reading. However, I encourage you to persevere in reading and be open enough to let facts change your perception. Then maybe, just maybe, you become convinced that Jesus Christ is more than just a good teacher or another prophet.

Let's begin our discovery by looking at Old and New Testament artefacts, which indicate that the Bible is historically accurate. Although we do not have originals, we do have over 5800 copies of the New Testament manuscripts. By far, this is the highest number of any ancient manuscripts available today! The preservation over time is remarkable when compared to other literary works. Like the Bible, we don't have any original document of Greek ancient literature, but Homer's Illiad, an epic 8th-century poem, is the second-best, with only 1757 copies. Greek philosopher Aristotle follows with 49 and Plato 7 copies. [10]

The early copies of scripture would have been created by devout Jews, who were keenly aware of the need for extreme care and accuracy in ancient times. The Jews knew that they were dealing with the Word of God, so they would even "wipe their pen clean before writing the name of God, counting the letters of both the original and the one being

---

[10] RightNow Media. (2019). Apologetics Quick Guide: Examining The Evidence For Christianity [Video]. Retrieved from: https://www.rightnowmedia.org/Content/Series/329795?episode=3

copied.” [11] The New Testament can be reproduced with 99.5% accuracy based upon the ancient copies, according to Bruce Metzger of Princeton Theological Seminary. The 0.5% that cannot be reproduced does not change the doctrine or belief in Christianity. For instance, some of the manuscripts might use “Christ Jesus” instead of “Jesus Christ”, but there is no doubt in their intention. In short, the scribes did a remarkable job in the transmission of the text that we now use today in the Bible over thousands of years.

Actually, in the ancient world, there has never been any debate on whether Jesus of Nazareth was a historical figure. [12] We know that Jesus came to earth 2000 years ago from Christian sources as well as non-Christian historical records. Based upon eyewitness accounts, we know where he lived, what he did and how he died. Shortly before the death of

---

[11] Backhaus, S., 2007. Jewish and Masoretic Rules for Copying the Scripture. [online] Riverviewbc.com. Available at: https://riverviewbc.com/wp-content/uploads/Jewish-and-Masoretic-Rules-for-Copying-the-Scripture.pdf [Accessed 4 April 2021]

[12] Gathercole, S. (2017). What is the historical evidence that Jesus Christ lived and died?. Retrieved 3 April 2021, from: https://www.theguardian.com/world/2017/apr/14/what-is-the-historical-evidence-that-jesus-christ-lived-and-died

Herod the Great, the King of Judea, Jesus was born in Bethlehem to Joseph and Mary. We know that Mary was a virgin when Jesus was conceived and that she "was found to be with child from the Holy Spirit" according to Matthew 1:18 and Luke 1:35. We know Joseph and the family fled to Egypt to protect baby Jesus when King Herod ordered the killing of all infants two years old and younger. They later returned and settled in Nazareth, a city in Galilee, where Jesus grew up. The Bible tells us that Jesus was the oldest of probably at least seven children. Jesus' earthly father was a carpenter, and that Jesus was deeply spiritual as he grew up, making an appearance at the temple with Jewish leaders at the age of 12. Not much else is known about Jesus until his public ministry began 18 years later.

The life and ministry of Jesus are primarily recorded in the four New Testament Gospel books, called Matthew, Mark, Luke and John. The Gospels have an overlap in stories and content, particularly related to the life and ministry of Jesus, but each is told from a different perspective. It is widely accepted that Matthew and John were two of the original twelve disciples chosen by Jesus, so they were eyewitnesses and knew Jesus. However, Luke and Mark were apostolic men with close affiliations with eyewitnesses.

Matthew was a tax collector, educated, and fluent in Greek, which was the original language used in the New Testament. The author of the Gospel of Matthew is never specifically mentioned by name in scripture, but the book seeks to establish Jesus' identity by giving us his genealogy and the references to Jesus being the fulfilment of the Old Testaments' prophecies as the long-awaited Messiah.

John was called the "beloved disciple", the youngest of the twelve disciples, and he was present when Jesus was crucified. In fact, on the cross, Jesus entrusted the care of His mother to the apostle John as recorded in John 19:26-27 with "When Jesus saw his mother there, and the disciple whom he loved standing nearby, he said to his mother, 'Dear woman, here is your son.' and to the disciple, 'Here is your mother.' From that time on, John took her into his home."

The Gospel of Luke made extensive use of eyewitness accounts, which is mentioned at the very beginning of the book in Luke 1:1-2. Although the author is not mentioned in the Gospel, it is likely written by Luke, who was a physician and the only non-Jew to write in the New Testament. The

Gospel of Luke concentrates on the life, death and resurrection of Jesus and ends with His ascension into heaven. Although the author of a book called Acts is also unknown, it begins with the ascension and tells of the early establishments of the Church and Christianity. It is thought that Luke may have authored Acts as well, with those two books making up more than 25% of the New Testament. The other half of the 27 books in the New Testament were either authored or attributed to an early evangelist named Paul, who was a friend of Luke. In a dramatic encounter and conversion on the road to Damascus, Paul had gone from someone who had persecuted Christians to a Greek-speaking Jew witnessing to the Gentiles about Jesus.

Mark's Gospel concentrates on Simon Peter's recollection of what he saw and heard from Jesus. He was a very close disciple of Jesus. Peter was a witness to Jesus' crucifixion and the empty tomb. He features prominently throughout the life of Jesus, with stories of Peter being the spokesman of the twelve disciples and the first to call Jesus the Messiah to his face. As you can see, every one of these Gospel authors was uniquely positioned to give a detailed, historical account with different perspectives. They weren't men just making up stories and fabrications because they were either eyewitnesses themselves or learned from accounts of people who actually knew Jesus.

In February 2009, our local church, The International Community Church, had the opportunity to tour the Holy Land in Israel. It was incredibly impactful to see so many of the archaeological discoveries and several places referenced in the Bible. An entire lifetime of study wouldn't be enough to absorb all that is now known about the people, places and events in the Bible, so my few references will be far from adequate for the evidence that exists. However, I hope that it gives you a sense of just how far-reaching the evidence is that supports the truth in the Bible.

It was hard to visit Israel and not feel moved by what we saw. There was so much to see, learn and experience, and it was especially impactful to be walking on the same land where Jesus Christ lived, preached, healed, died and rose to a new life. It drew me to a new level of encountering the living God in my own faith, as we visited the following places:

Place of Interest	Biblical Significance
Nazareth	Jesus spent most of his youth here.
Cana	Site of Jesus' first miracle – turning water into wine.
Sea of Galilee	Much of Jesus's ministry took place on the northern shore.
Gethsemane	Very likely where Jesus agonised over his impending crucifixion.
Mount of Olives	Overlooks Temple Mount in Jerusalem; likely where Jesus will return.
Megiddo	Prophesized in Revelation to be the site for the future Armageddon (the end of the world)
Qumran	Site where the Dead Sea Scrolls were found
Caesarea	Built by Herod the Great for Caesar

Mount of Beatitudes	Probable site for Jesus' Sermon on the Mount (Matt 5:1-12)
Dead Sea	World's lowest place on earth and incredibly salty water
Jerusalem	Considered the holy city by Jews, Christians and Muslims

Whole books have been written about the archaeological discoveries from the Old and New Testament times. "There have been more than 30,000 discoveries which relate to the Bible", according to John Mc Ray, who had supervised evacuating teams in the Holy Land. Even in the vast amount of discoveries, there has not been anything that contradicts the truth in the Bible. [13]

Did you catch that fact? Not one archaeological discovery has ever been contrary to the Bible! In fact,

---

[13] RightNow Media. (2019). Apologetics Quick Guide: Examining The Evidence For Christianity [Video]. Retrieved from: https://www.rightnowmedia.org/Content/Series/329795?episode=3

Christianity is the only world religion that can be substantiated with archaeological evidence.

You might be wondering how do we know whether the modern-day copies of the Bible compare to the original Hebrew scripture? After all, the scriptures have been copied so many times over thousands of years. A Bedouin shepherd boy discovered one of the greatest finds to authenticate the Bible in 1947 in Qumran, Israel. He was looking for a lost goat and tossed a stone in a cave, which hit a clay pot containing a portion of what we now refer to as the Dead Sea Scrolls. Prior to the discovery, all that was available was the Masoretic text, universally accepted as the authentic Hebrew Bible, written in 900 AD, after the life of Jesus. Remarkably, the Dead Sea Scrolls predate the Masoretic text by almost 1000 years and are written in Hebrew, Aramaic and a few other languages. They contain every book of the Old Testament, except for the Book of Esther. The Dead Sea Scrolls are believed to have been written by the Essenes, a Jewish group who left Palestinian society for a more monastic lifestyle in the wilderness.

They are the largest, and in most cases, the earliest, examples of various parts of biblical texts. [14] [15] Even though 1000 years separate those two texts, the transmission of the original Hebrew text is remarkably precise and accurate.

I was recently listening to a high profile trial, watching the prosecutors ask each of the witnesses to identify themselves using video footage. Obviously, we cannot do the same to prove the veracity of the Bible since video footage wasn't used in ancient times, but we can use archaeological evidence to prove Old Testament Biblical characters existed. Remarkably, a House of David inscription on a black basalt slab was discovered in 1993. It dates to the 9th century BC, and it is the earliest mention of King David outside of the Bible. King David reigned for 40 years over Israel, and he is mentioned in 1 Kings 2:11. It

---

[14] McDowell, J. and McDowell, S., 2017. Evidence That Demands A Verdict. Nashville: Thomas Nelson Publishers. Page 57 of 361, Loc 1831 of 11386 by Josh McDowell

[15] Maeir, A. (2019). Digging for the Bible: 10 key discoveries from the Holy Land. Retrieved 3 April 2021, from: https://www.historyextra.com/period/ancient-history/digging-bible-key-discoveries-archaeology-holy-land-dead-sea-scrolls/

permanently resides in the Israel Museum in Jerusalem. [16] [17]

Also, The Cylinder of Nabonidus was discovered in 1854 in Iraq and is on display in the British Museum. It mentions Belshazzar (died 539 BC), who is recorded in Daniel 5 as the last King of Babylon. [18] Christians might recognise this King as the one who held a banquet, and the prophet, Daniel, was called to interpret the handwriting on the wall, which predicted Babylon might fall to the Persians. These discoveries mean King David and Belshazzar were real, living men who are referred to in the Old Testament,

---

[16] Maugh II, T. (1993). Stone Tablet Offers 1st Physical Evidence of Biblical King David : Archeology: Researchers say 13 lines of Aramaic script confirm the battle for Tel Dan recounted in the Bible, marking a victory by Asa of the House of David. Retrieved 3 April 2021, from: https://www.latimes.com/archives/la-xpm-1993-08-14-me-23862-story.html

[17] Bible-history.com. 2020. Bible History Online - House of David Inscription (Biblical Archaeology). [online] Available at: https://www.bible-history.com/archaeology/israel/house-of-david-inscription.html [Accessed 3 April 2021].

[18] McGee, M. (2015). Convince Me There's A God – Archaeology 26. Retrieved 3 April 2021, from: https://faithandselfdefense.com/2015/08/15/convince-me-theres-a-god-archaeology-26/

even before Christ. These are only a couple of examples of the remarkable Old Testament discoveries.

Now, let's turn our attention to some of the findings for the New Testament. Several papyri had been found in this regard, dating back to the earliest versions of the New Testament. Papyri are thicker ancient materials, like paper, which were used in Egypt. For example, the Chester Beatty Papyri, housed primarily in Dublin and the University of Michigan, contains most of the New Testament and dates about 250 AD. The Bodmer Papyrus, discovered in Egypt in 1952, contains most of the Gospel of John, which was written about 200 AD. The John Rylands fragment contains a piece from John 18, found in Egypt, which dates to 125 AD. John was the last of the Gospels to be written, and we know that the Gospel of John was not written in Egypt. That implies the Gospel of John had to be written well before this date, pushing more of the Gospels into the 1st century, the same century in which Jesus lived, which adds credibility to the text.

Quotes from early church leaders also help to establish the timing and existence of books in the New Testament. Polycarp, bishop of Smyrna, wrote letters to other Christians in 110 AD and quoted all four Gospels and the majority of Paul's Epistles. Ignatius, bishop of Antioch, quoted 24 different books from the New Testament. Clement, bishop of Rome, was writing in 95 AD, and he quoted from 3 out of 4 of the Gospels. This means the four Gospels had to be written before this time in the first century.

It would be entirely reasonable to expect significant historical events to appear in ancient manuscripts. For example, if someone was documenting US history for the year 2011, you would expect the mention of the September 11th tragedy, since that was the single largest terrorist event in history. We know that the writer of Luke and Acts focuses his writing around the city of Jerusalem. Acts 1:8 says, "You will be my witnesses in the Jerusalem, and in all Judea and Samaria, and to the ends of the earth." However, what is not included in either of the two books is the destruction of the temple when the Romans captured the city from the Jews in 70 AD. By not including such a significant event, we are led to believe that Luke and Acts were written well before this time and in the same century of Jesus Christ. This means eyewitnesses were alive when the documents were written about Jesus, which gives it even more credibility. [19]

"The first Christian writings to talk about Jesus, are the epistles of St Paul, and scholars agree that the earliest of these letters were written within 25 years of Jesus's death at the very latest, while the detailed biographical accounts of Jesus in the New Testament gospels date from around 40 years after he died. All of these appeared within the lifetimes of numerous eyewitnesses and provide descriptions that are consistent with the culture and geography of first-century Palestine." [20]

On our Holy Land trip, we saw Caesarea Maritima, which was a palace built by Herod the Great, on the coast of Israel. There, archaeologists found the Pontius Pilate Stone inscription. Pilate was the ruler of Israel, and he condemned Jesus to death. This discovery confirms Pilate's existence

---

[19] RightNow Media. (2019). Apologetics Quick Guide: Examining The Evidence For Christianity [Video]. Retrieved from: https://www.rightnowmedia.org/Content/Series/329795?episode=3

[20] Gathercole, S. (2017). What is the historical evidence that Jesus Christ lived and died?. Retrieved 3 April 2021, from: https://www.theguardian.com/world/2017/apr/14/what-is-the-historical-evidence-that-jesus-christ-lived-and-died

and his office. In John 9:1-12, we read the story of Jesus healing a man blind by birth. Christ spits on the ground, makes some mud and puts it on the blind man's eyes. He then instructs the blind man to wash in the Pool of Siloam. The blind man does so and is healed. In the third century AD, a church was built above a pool attached to Hezekiah's water tunnel in Jerusalem to commemorate the healing of the blind man reported in John's Gospel. Until recently, this was thought to be the Pool of Siloam. However, during sewerage works in 2004, engineers stumbled upon the steps of a first-century ritual pool near the mouth of Hezekiah's tunnel. By the summer of 2005, archaeologists said it was, without any doubt, the missing Pool of Siloam. Mark D Roberts reports, "In the plaster of this pool were found coins that establish the date of the pool to the years before and after Jesus. There is little question that this is in fact the Pool of Siloam, to which Jesus sent the blind man in John 9." [21]

---

[21] Williams, P., 2010. Questions | Uncover. [online] Uncover.org.uk. Available at: https://www.uncover.org.uk/questions/does-archaeology-confirm-the-new-testament/ [Accessed 3 April 2021]

Now, let's explore some of the secular evidence related to Jesus. These include writings outside of the scripture, which help to demonstrate the truth contained in the Bible, and specifically what is said about Jesus in the Gospels. We know that within a few decades of his lifetime, Jesus had been mentioned by Jewish and Roman historians in their non-biblical writings. A Jewish first-century historian named Flavius Josephus (37-100 AD) made a direct reference to James, "the brother of Jesus, the so-called Christ" in Jewish Antiquities of the Jews around 94 AD. Josephus' writings also refer to the life of Christ, crucifixion, and persecution of the disciples.

About 20 years after Josephus, we know Roman politicians Cornelius Tacitus (55-117 AD) and Pliny made a reference to Christ in their secular writings. Tacitus talked about the crucifixion of Christ in Annals, book 15, chapter 44, in the following lines, "Christus, the founder of the name, was put to death by Pontius Pilate." This is one of the earliest non-Christian references. From Tacitus, we learn that Jesus was executed while Pontius Pilate was the Roman prefect in charge of Judea (26-36 AD) and Tiberius was the emperor

(14-37 AD). These reports fit with the timeframe of the gospels.

Also, around 112 AD, Pliny the Younger wrote to the emperor Trajan in a letter called Epistles X.96., seeking counsel on how to treat the Christians by saying he "made them curse Christ, which a genuine Christian cannot be induced to do." Essentially, the Christians, even though they were being persecuted, would not deny Christ. We know that when Pliny was governor in modern-day northern Turkey, Christians worshipped Christ as a God. In addition, we have several other first and second-century non-biblical sources, Jews and Gentiles, such as Thallus a Samaria historian (52 A.D.), Tertullian, Suetonius the Roman historian (120 A.D.) and Lucian Greek Satirist (2nd century), which make references about the Christians, the darkness that occurred at the crucifixion and the man who was crucified in Palestine.

[22] [23] All of this is consistent with the Bible and what reportedly happened at the crucifixion of Christ.

By using only secular testimony, we can substantiate that "Jesus was crucified by Pontius Pilate at Passover time, the disciples believed that Jesus rose from the dead on the third day, the church leaders charged Jesus with sorcery, that Christianity could not be contained and spread into the Roman world, Nero and other Roman rulers persecuted the Christians, early Christians denied polytheism which is the belief in many gods, and that they lived lives dedicated to Christian teaching and worshipped Jesus Christ as God." [24] So, the secular testimony, which is currently available, is congruent to what has been written about Jesus in the Bible.

---

[22] McDowell, J. and McDowell, S., 2017. Evidence That Demands A Verdict. Nashville: Thomas Nelson Publishers. Page 81-84 of 361, Loc 2480,2494,2508, 2520, 2535, 2548 of 11386 by Josh McDowell
[23] RightNow Media. (2019). Apologetics Quick Guide: Examining The Evidence For Christianity [Video]. Retrieved from https://www.rightnowmedia.org/Content/Series/329795?episode=3
[24] RightNow Media. (2019). Apologetics Quick Guide: Examining The Evidence For Christianity [Video]. Retrieved from: https://www.rightnowmedia.org/Content/Series/329795?episode=3

Hopefully, you agree that the vast amount of archaeological evidence and the various non-Christian sources make a convincing case for the truth of the Bible and the facts known about Jesus Christ. Believing in Jesus is not blind faith; rather, it is backed by evidence. God has revealed himself through the truth in the Bible. He became flesh through His Son, Jesus Christ, and thankfully, God continues to work in our lives today through the power of the Holy Spirit.

Chapter 5: Who Do You Say I Am?

Tiny and fragile. No bigger than our hand. Our daughter entered the world unexpectedly nine weeks earlier. Eight weeks later, she was finally able to come home. It was a rocky start to life, for her and us, as parents. Our daughter spent the first year attached to a heart monitor, with home health care representatives coming to our house regularly to ensure we could perform cardiac pulmonary resuscitation (CPR), if required. Her heart monitor was there to alert us to start interventions in case she quit breathing. Before every feeding, we needed to give her medicine 30 minutes ahead of time to help control an undeveloped valve over her stomach. Needless to say, we were badly sleep deprived during the first year of her life. However, that tiny baby has grown into a strong, fiercely passionate, creative young lady as of today. As her Dad described at her wedding, our daughter doesn't just draw you a picture; she can paint it and make it come alive in technicolour.

Just like our daughter, hearts are a life source that nobody can do without. Our hearts always seem to beat just a little faster and harder for our passions and pursuits. In Matthew 6:21, it says, "For where your treasure is, there your heart will be also." I pray that you come to believe that Jesus Christ is the one and only Messiah and that you will treasure Him with all your heart. Jesus is the one foretold in the Old Testament scriptures and the one proclaimed throughout the New Testament in the Father, Son and Holy Spirit. If Jesus is our Lord and Saviour, then His values will be reflected in how we live, use our money and spend our time. Every Christian needs a burning passion for knowing Him and making Him known in our life-long pursuits.

In the late 1600s, a lady named Suzanna Wesley was extremely busy running her home and schooling her 19 children while also giving each of them a devout spiritual upbringing. Each child was required to learn Latin and Greek and memorise major portions of the New Testament. One of her sons, John Wesley, later became the founder of the Methodist Church. Every day for an hour, Suzanna would put the apron over her head to pray. The children knew not to disturb the mother during this precious time with her

Heavenly Father. In the midst of a busy life, Suzanna Wesley prioritised spending time with God. [25]

Unlike Suzanna, my daily quiet time with God does not involve an apron over my head, but it does include spending time in prayer, actively seeking what He may want to say to me, meditating on verses from the Bible, reading daily devotionals, and worshipping Him. From those precious moments with God, I know that He loves me unconditionally and that I can rest in His mighty, sovereign grace. Regardless of my circumstances, I can rejoice that with God, all things are possible and that He is at work in my life. He is faithful in the midst of every trial, with perfect timing. Day by day, I bow my head to walk, talk and rely upon Jesus Christ. He reigns, sovereign over all, and most importantly, came to give me everlasting life.

A little over two thousand years ago, Jesus made His entrance to the world in an unexpected way, as a tiny baby

---

[25] Fanny Crosby: America's Hymn Queen. (2021). Retrieved 3 April 2021, from: https://www.christianity.com/church/church-history/timeline/1801-1900/fanny-crosby-americas-hymn-queen-11630385.html

born in the little town of Bethlehem to a Jewish couple. His very name, Jesus, derived from the Hebrew name Yeshua, means "to deliver; to rescue." It conveys His mission and purpose for coming into this world, which was to secure everlasting life for each of us. Jesus came to save mankind and each of us by being the sinless sacrifice so that we could be assured everlasting life. For centuries, Israel had expected a Messiah to free them from Roman bondage and oppression. Jesus was not just a Good Teacher, as the Jews believed. Jesus was the long-awaited Messiah, the Son of Man, the Son of God and the King of the Jews.

Jesus stepped down from heaven into this world, as fully human and fully divine. As Thomas Schultz says, "Not one recognised religious leader, not Moses, Paul, Buddha, Mohammed, Confucius, etc. has ever claimed to be God; that is, with the exception of Jesus Christ. Christ is the only religious leader who has ever claimed to be a deity." [26]

---

[26] Schultz, T., The Doctrine of the Person of Christ with an Emphasis upon the Hypostatic Union (DTS dissertation, 1962), 209. Retrieved from: https://beliefmap.org/jesus-shines

At His trial before the crucifixion, the Jews challenged Jesus on His claim of being God. Jesus made a very clear proclamation before the Jews in John 8:58b with the statement, "before Abraham was born, I am!" This infuriated them because they believed that only God could be the "I am", which was a term used in the Old Testament scriptures and commonly associated with God. In the end, Jesus was crucified because of His claim to be God, instead of His actions, because He never committed a sin.

The Gospels tell us about the life of Jesus Christ, but Christ has always existed, even from the beginning of time. Even before the Gospels were written, the Old Testament scriptures and prophets told us that Jesus would be: born in Bethlehem to a virgin, descendant of King David, called a Nazarene, hated without cause, crucified with criminals, resurrected from the dead, and ascended into heaven and seated at the right of God the Father. From the Scriptures, we have very specific details about Jesus' death on the cross, such as He would be given vinegar to drink, his side would be pierced, his bones would not be broken, and that soldiers would gamble for his garments. The many prophecies range from the very beginning of the Bible in Genesis and are later fulfilled with the coming of Jesus in the New Testament.

Jesus fulfilled the prophecies with His coming, yet many at that time still thought He was nothing more than another prophet or a good teacher. There's a particularly poignant moment when Jesus asks His disciples, "Who do people say the Son of Man is?" in Matthew 16:13-15. They replied, "Some say John the Baptist; others say Elijah; and still others, Jeremiah or one of the prophets." John the Baptist, Elijah and Jeremiah were all prophets, and it would be entirely typical for the Jews to say that Jesus was just another prophet. However, Jesus goes further by asking the disciples, "But what about you?" he asked. "Who do you say I am?" In all of Scripture, this has to be one of my all-time favourite verses because it indicates that the choice to follow Jesus is always individualised and personal to each of us. Each of us has to answer whether we believe in Christ. Jesus is asking the disciples, his closest friends, the people who have seen him perform numerous miracles, "Who do you say I am?" In verse 16, Simon Peter, one of the disciples, answers, "You are the Christ, the Son of the living God." Yes, that is exactly who Jesus is, the Messiah, the Son of the living God, and I'm thrilled to say that He is also my Lord and Saviour.

Before Jesus was crucified, he appeared before the High Priest Caiaphas to be tried for blasphemy for claiming to be God. In Mark 14:61b-62, Caiaphas asks Jesus, "Are you the Christ, the Son of the Blessed One?" "I am," said Jesus. "And you will see the Son of Man sitting at the right hand of the Mighty One and coming on the clouds of heaven." Caiaphas and the whole Sanhedrin, a Jewish high court, knew the Scriptures, and there was no possibility of misunderstanding. Jesus was claiming that he was "the Son of Man" and "coming with the clouds of heaven" as prophesized in Daniel 7:13. The account in Mark 14 continues by saying that the High Priest tore his clothes and said in verse 64, "You have heard the blasphemy. What do you think?" They all condemned him as worthy of death.

There's only one Caiaphas that we know from history, and he was the High Priest, the one who condemned Jesus to death. In 1990, the Caiaphas Ossuary was found; inscribed on the side was, "Joseph, son of Caiaphas", which used to be the proper name of Caiaphas. We not only know that Caiaphas existed, but we also have the bones of the 60-year-old male. [27] Once again, the archaeological findings are congruent with the events in the Bible.

Jesus showed the world His power and authority through miracles. The blind received sight, the lame walked, the deaf were granted hearing, the seas were calmed, and the dead were raised through Jesus. His miracles were done in public with witnesses, and they demonstrated a wide variety of powers. Each of the miracles had a purpose, which was to reveal Jesus' authority and show God's power.

Some unbelievers wonder why they don't see more miracles today. But, Paul Little reminds us that "Miracles are not necessary for us today as a basis of faith in Christ, because we have extraordinary records of superior accuracy to show us God's truth…Every court in the world operates on the basis of reliable testimony by word of mouth or in writing." The Bible is God's revealed truth to all of us. Does God still perform miracles today? Yes, of course, He does, but we should never forget that we also have a detailed

---

[27] RightNow Media. (2019). Apologetics Quick Guide: Examining The Evidence For Christianity [Video]. Retrieved from: https://www.rightnowmedia.org/Content/Series/329795?episode=3

record of all the miracles that Jesus has already done in the Bible.

On the final night before Jesus was crucified, he had gathered his disciples to have one last meal. Christians refer to this as the Last Supper. At that meal, Jesus shared some very important promises with the disciples, one of them was regarding the Holy Spirit. Jesus promised the disciples that they would do even greater things than he had done, as referenced in John 14:12, "What I'm about to tell you is true. Anyone who has faith in Me will do what I have been doing. In fact, he will do even greater things. That is because I am going to the Father." The second promise is that Jesus would send the Holy Spirit to reside in each of them, according to John 16:5-7, "Now I am going to him who sent me [Heavenly Father], yet none of you asks me, 'Where are you going?' Because I have said these things, you are filled with grief. But I tell you the truth: It is for your good that I am going away. Unless I go away, the Counselor [Holy Spirit] will not come to you; but if I go, I will send him to you."

Admittedly, the triune nature of God is hard to understand. How can we have one God, in three distinct persons - God the Father, God the Son and the Holy Spirit?

At the very least, it demonstrates how God is beyond our human comprehensions. He is God, and we are not. Some things we will never know about Him. To some extent, we must accept this and walk by faith. For example, we all know that water can exist in three forms – ice, liquid and gas. We use all different forms of one oxygen and two hydrogen atoms, but very few of us could explain how that happens. What is most important is that we don't limit our faith to what we know about the Heavenly Father, the Son or the Holy Spirit. Instead, we need to be willing to be obedient to God's will and ask Him to mightily use us for His glory. With this important context, let's dive into what the Bible says about the Holy Spirit.

Christianity is a monotheist religion believing in one God but experienced as three distinct persons – God the Father, God the Son and the Holy Spirit. Sometimes you will hear it represented as "The Trinity" for the Father, Son and Holy Spirit. Although the Trinity is never used as a term in the Bible, we know all three were there when the world was created, and the understanding is reflected throughout the Bible. Christians believe in one God, co-equals in deity, with the Father, Son and Holy Spirit taking on different roles.

God the Father was the first person to build a relationship with the Israelites. He led them for thousands of years, which is recorded in the Old Testament, the first 39 books of the Bible. He also encouraged them to follow His law, which served to make them aware of their sin.

Jesus, or God the Son, was the second person of the Trinity. He began a relationship with mankind when He was born in the manger. Jesus walked among us, fully man and fully God. He performed miracles, showing His authority and power overall. Jesus, as "God in the flesh", lived a sinless life. Thereby, Jesus was the perfect sacrifice, once for all as referenced in John 3:17, when it says, "For God did not send his Son into the world to condemn the world, but to save the world through him." Jesus was tortured and killed by the Romans on a cross, but He proved his deity by rising from the dead on the 3rd day, on what all Christians celebrate as Easter Sunday. Jesus had claimed that He was God when He was sentenced at his trial before the crucifixion. Indeed, He proved that He was God and that He could conquer all things, even death, by rising from the grave.

On the eve of his death, Jesus promised the disciples, "But you will receive power when the Holy Spirit comes on you" (Acts 1:8). After Jesus ascended into heaven, the perpetual, empowering presence of the Holy Spirit did come to indwell the disciples and, as a matter of fact, resides in all Christians upon their confession of faith (Eph 1:13). The third person of the Trinity is the Holy Spirit. Before Jesus ascended back into heaven, He sent a "comforter" or "advocate" that will be with us forever, in John 14:16-17.

The Holy Spirit points us back to God's Word and reminds us of all that Jesus said and did as in John 14:26, "But the Advocate, the Holy Spirit, whom the Father will send in my name, will teach you all things and will remind you of everything I have said to you." The Holy Spirit first began his relationship with humans when he descended upon the 1st-century church believers as "tongues of fire" during Pentecost in Acts 2. The Bible says that Jesus, God the Father and the Holy Spirit are one. Therefore, when we reference having a relationship with Jesus, we really mean having a relationship with God the Father and the Holy Spirit as well. [28]

---

[28] Michelle, A., n.d. What Is a Personal Relationship with Jesus? (And How to Know God Personally). [online] Vibrant Christian Living.

Benny Hinn tries to explain the Trinity by giving us an illustration of turning on a light with three forces involved. There is one who gives the command. One who walks up to the switch and flips it on or performs the command. But ultimately, it is the electricity that is the power to produce the light. 'If you need light, to whom do you turn? You look to the Father because He is the giver of every good and perfect gift…the source is the Father. But the giver of that source is Christ, and the power of the source is the Holy Spirit. The Father "operates". The Son "administrates". The Holy Spirit "manifests the administration of the operation". [29][30]

"From the moment you accept Jesus as Saviour, it is the Spirit that gives you the will, the strength and the desire to obey God and live the Christian life. Without Him, it is impossible." [31] When we commit our life to Christ, we lay

---

Available at: https://vibrantchristianliving.com/personal-relationship-with-jesus/ [Accessed 3 April 2021]
[29] Hinn, B., 2014. Good Morning Holy Spirit. Nashville, Tennessee: Thomas Nelson, p.49
[30] Ibid, pg. 139
[31] Ibid, pg. 168

aside our reliance upon ourselves and walk in freedom and power of the Holy Spirit, who works in and through each of us.

God is the creator of the universe, an enabler of everlasting life through the Son, Jesus Christ, and a helper or intercessor with the ever-present Holy Spirit in the life of every Christian. The Holy Spirit has been present since the beginning in Genesis 1:2, when the "Spirit of God was hovering over the waters". There are other examples in the Old Testament, where the Spirit anoints specific people for special purposes, such as Gideon and Samson, to defeat enemies of the Israelites. We also see the Spirit present with Bezalel in the construction of the tabernacle and with King David, the 2nd king of Israel. The Old Testament book of Joel 2:28 even prophecies "I will pour out my Spirit on all people", which is later fulfilled in the New Testament. More directly, we see the Holy Spirit in the New Testament at Jesus baptism (Matthew 3:13-17), descending upon people at Pentecost (Acts 2) and working during the sanctification process, as God makes us more holy (1 Peter 1:2, 2 Thessalonians 2:13). [32]

The bottom line is we need to walk by faith, knowing that we will never be able to understand all the ways in which God works on this side of heaven. However, we can walk assured that the Holy Spirit lives and resides in each one of us once we make a decision to follow Christ. He is our helper and advocate. When God calls us to do something, then he will equip us for the task through the power of the Spirit.

Esther Ahn Kim lived during WWII, during the Japanese occupation of Korea. She refused to bow down at the shrines in every corner of her country and was imprisoned from 1939 to 1945. While preparing for prison, she ate decaying food, knowing that she would be served that while she was detained. She memorised more than 100 chapters from the Bible and many hymns because she knew that she would not be able to keep her Bible. She learned to recognise the voice

---

[32] Cherrett, L., n.d. Bible Q&A: Does the Holy Spirit get mentioned before the Day of Pentecost, and in the Old Testament?. [online] Biblesociety.org.uk. Available at: https://www.biblesociety.org.uk/explore-the-bible/bible-articles/bible-qa-holy-spirit-in-the-bible/ [Accessed 4 April 2021].

of the Holy Spirit and was filled with love for people. While in prison, Esther was used in countless instances to spread the Good News of Christ, including to the prisoners, jailers and government officials. Esther was "ready every day and every moment, asking God, 'Who do you want me to love for you today?'' [33] What a testimony of someone who not only knew Christ but was willing to make Him known to others through loving them in the midst of their circumstances!

[33] Chan, F. and Yankoski, D., 2009. Forgotten God. 1st ed. Colorado Springs, CO: David C Cook, pp.97 of 193, Loc 906 of 1755.

Chapter 6: Walking in Relationship With Jesus Christ

We were 21 years old when we married. I had just graduated from college, and my husband, Kevin, had one semester left at Texas A&M University. We had been engaged for two years. My parents wouldn't allow us to marry before I had my degree. I had hurried through as fast as I could and graduated a semester early, so we could finally get married. With thousands of students walking across the graduation stage, my parents had no problem identifying me. I had spelt out MRS DEGREE on my graduation mortarboard cap because we were finally going to get married two weeks after my graduation. With a borrowed dress and a total of $500 between us, we married just after Christmas, during the semester break. Those early days are fleeting memories, although that may be a blessing because some of those moments we wouldn't want to relive with rust running out of the water pipes, dark brown shag carpet and no air conditioning in boiling Texas heat.

Back in 1984, weddings were far more simple than they are today, with typically a short ceremony followed by a punch and cake reception. It wasn't possible to videotape or live stream weddings because the internet didn't even exist back in those "dinosaur days". However, the church where we got married did have the ability to record an audio cassette tape. Fast forward, after moving 23 times in 36 years, and it was finally time to unload a storage facility in Houston, Texas. It had been crated shut for 17 of the years that we were living in England. We felt like we were on a large treasure hunt as we eagerly unwrapped the enormous packing paper to reveal what was there. Most of what was in storage were sentimental family heirlooms, probably worthless to anyone else but important to us.

Let me assure you that after all of our house moves, you get less sentimental and definitely less interested in moving unnecessary stuff around. However, we did manage to keep the very poorly lit pictures of our wedding and the audio cassette, which was one of the treasures found in storage. After all of these years, we wondered what we might be able to salvage from that audio cassette. Could either of us remember the songs that were played at our wedding? Sadly, no, but we did remember a beautiful trumpet duet opened the wedding processional, followed by The Lord's Prayer as the closing song. Other than that, we didn't recall many other details.

We took our wedding cassette to a video professional to find out if they could convert it to a digital format. Some of it had badly deteriorated, but remarkably, they were able to salvage most of it. After all of the decades of time, my husband and I enjoyed listening to the vows that we had made. We laughed again when we heard the pastor read the wrong passage in Ruth. The pastor was supposed to read an endearing statement of loyalty and commitment in Ruth 1:16b, "Where you go I will go, and where you stay I will stay. Your people will be my people and your God my God." Instead, during our wedding, the pastor read Ruth 2:15, "Even if she gathers among the sheaves, don't reprimand her." Standing at the altar, we knew it was a mistake, but at that moment, all that really mattered was the fateful words, "I do".

Like all couples, we've been through some highs and lows throughout our many years of marriage. The depth of our relationship has grown over time. We've celebrated life's wonderful moments of the birth of our children. We have seen our children grow, mature and marry their spouses. We have known the depth of the sorrow involved with losing ageing parents and the miscarriage of a child. We've seen the stress caused by unemployment, jobs and the premature birth of our daughter. We have even witnessed the fragility of life through accidents, health crisis, hurricanes and most recently, the worldwide pandemic. My husband and I fully agree that all of these times and experiences have strengthened the depth of our relationship and marriage. It is much the same with our Heavenly Father. As we spend time and live through different experiences with Jesus Christ, our relationship matures and develops. But, how do we really have a relationship with Jesus when we cannot see Him?

In order for us to have a relationship and grow spiritually, we must first make a decision to follow Jesus Christ as our Lord and Saviour. We must believe that our sin has separated us from God but that Jesus died on the cross and overcame death so that we might receive eternal life. God's provision for our sin was through the sacrifice of His only Son, Jesus. Romans 5:8 says, "But God demonstrates his own love for us in this: While we were still sinners, Christ died for us." From cover to cover, the Bible reiterates God's love and His desire for a relationship with each of us. We don't have to be perfect. And, we don't have to wait until we manage to get our life together. We just need to come, as we are, knowing His grace is more than enough to forgive our sins.

We must be willing to set aside our own plans to be led and obedient to Christ. If this is your desire, then you can start your journey by saying a prayer, similar to this,

"God, I recognise that I'm not perfect and that I am sorry for my sins. I ask for your forgiveness. I accept that your death on the cross was for my sins, and through your resurrection, I can be assured of everlasting life. From this day forward, I want you to be my Lord and Saviour, with my life being led by you. Amen."

If this reflects the desires of your heart and you prayed something similar, then you now have a personal relationship with Christ. Your salvation is only made possible through your belief in Jesus Christ, and there is no other way that you can have everlasting life. You must believe in Jesus and what He did for you. As 1 John 5:11b says, "God has given us eternal life, and this life is in His Son." Once you make a decision to follow Christ, then your old nature, which is dominated by sin, is replaced with a new nature per 2 Corinthians 5:17. With a new nature, we begin to have a Godly perspective in our choices and decisions. This may mean that we also have to make some lifestyle changes to align with what Christ would expect of us. To walk in a relationship with Jesus will be a lifelong journey as you read and apply God's Word.

Once you declare your faith, you are a new creation in Christ, but most certainly, the transformation will take time to become more like Him. As Christians, we are forgiven when we confess our sins, but sometimes old habits are hard to break. Trust that God is going to continue making you more and more like Him through the Holy Spirit. Seek out a Bible-teaching church with other believers to help you grow and mature spiritually. Regularly set aside time each day to pray and read the Bible. Examine your life to see what doesn't align with Jesus' teachings and ask the Holy Spirit to help you actively take steps to make those changes. Learn to decipher when God speaks to you because He intends for us to be led and guided by Him. Most importantly, let go of your past and walk in the freedom of God's saving grace, knowing that your eternal future is now secure.

Remember we started with a story about Mr McCunn, who went on the Alaskan adventure but never returned. He may not physically be with us today, but his 100-page diary left a lasting clue about his profession of faith. In the diary, it had, "Dear God in heaven, please forgive me my weakness and sins. Please look over my family." [34]

I praise God that it sounds like Mr McCunn had made the decision to follow Christ, and more than anything, I want that for you. Only you and God know whether you are confident about your eternal destination being heaven.

We have reached the end of our time together. I pray that this book has sufficiently conveyed that God loves you. God sent His only Son, Jesus Christ, to die for your sins and to guarantee everlasting life. I want you to know that the Bible is true and that you can rely on God's faithfulness. God is all-knowing, all-powerful and all-present everywhere. He has a plan and purpose for every one of us. And finally, that God wants to have a personal relationship with each of us through prayer.

---

[34] Thompson, Emily, et al. (2021). Death in the Wild - Carl McCunn • Morbidology. Retrieved 2 April 2021, from https://morbidology.com/death-in-the-wild-carl-mccunn/

When we pray, we are having a conversation with God, and this can be done anytime, anywhere. Will God always answer our prayers in the way that we want? Certainly not, but He always does what is best for us. We must accept that He is God, and we are not. God is delighted when we come to Him in prayer.

I will leave you with one last personal illustration of God at work in my own life through prayer. I had just flown into England from the States and had to run one quick errand in town. I was exhausted. As I drove into the town parking lot, I realised that I had absolutely no British coins for the parking meter. In a very humble manner, I bowed my head and prayed along these lines, "God, I know that you are able. I ask for you to just provide me with enough money to pay for my parking. I am completely exhausted and have no means of payment. Father, thank you for hearing me!" I parked my car and walked over to the parking meter machine. I slipped my hand into the coin dispenser to find a 50 pence piece, which was enough for one hour. In 17 years, I have never found a single pence in a parking pay machine in England, but that day, God provided it to me. At that moment, I knew there was a God who listened, answered and was at work in every detail of my life, and He wants to be at work in your life as well.

I pray this book has challenged you to seriously consider whether you are ready for heaven. If you are already walking with Jesus, then I praise God for your salvation. However, if you haven't given your life over to Jesus or if you are unsure, then I hope today is that day for all of eternity!

It would be my pleasure to encourage you in your faith. Please drop me a message at **TEBirdBooks@gmail.com** if you invited Jesus to be your Lord and Saviour today or if you would like me to pray with or for you. Most definitely, the best is yet to come if you believe in Jesus Christ! Let's be ready for heaven! God Bless You!

Thanks for reading! If you enjoyed this book, I would be grateful if you would please consider leaving a review on the site where you purchased it and joining my blog at http://www.TEBirdBooks.com.

Lightning Source UK Ltd.
Milton Keynes UK
UKHW020958100821
388622UK00015B/1205